ISBN No. 978-1-4067-8735-1

THE ART OF TAXIDERMY

BY
F. TOSE

TAXIDERMY

TAXIDERMY

ALTHOUGH it is true that the curing of skins for clothing has been practiced from the most remote times, the art of Taxidermy is of comparatively recent origin. The mounting of birds and other animals in natural and lifelike positions has been extensively practiced only during the last century.

It has been left until even more recent times to elevate the art from its crude beginnings. By combining the efforts of the taxidermist, artist and modeller, some really great works have been executed in the best museums of America and Europe. In our own country we have the commencement of several museums, one at Victoria, B. C., being fairly complete. Wonderful as our North American wild life is, many species are in various stages of the process of extinction and it is regrettable that they should be allowed to pass before their external characteristics go on permanent record through the taxidermist's skill.

This book is written expressly for the amateur. Let it be understood that its purpose is not to incite the would-be collector to go forth and slay everything in sight with the sole purpose of making a large collection of stuffed fauna. Far from it. The workshops of professional taxidermists are periodically filled with our most valuable birds, slain in many cases by alleged sportsmen who go after game and, finding none, must shoot something. There are many trophies secured by legitimate sport that can be preserved and will in later years bring back memories that cause us to live over again the scenes and exploits of vigorous youth. The practice of taxidermy is also a source of much pleasure and no little profit to those who attain proficiency in the art.

The observations and instructions contained in these pages are the outcome of many years practical experience and it is my sincere wish that they will prove of great assistance to those readers who are interested in this work.

Before we proceed further let me with all good intentions issue a word of warning against the indiscriminate killing of birds and many other forms of wild life, a great number of which are of the utmost economic importance to the agriculturist and the community at large. The Dominion Department of Agriculture, Ottawa and the United States Department of Agriculture, Washington, D. C., issue free bulletins written by specialists on these subjects. These can be had for the asking, and I would strongly advise readers to procure them and to make a study of the habits of the different forms of wild life in their vicinity. This will help greatly in the practice of Taxidermy, and to those who are farmers, will also eventually have an additional dollar and cent value by showing which forms are beneficial and which harmful.

TOOLS

The tools required by the Taxidermist need not be many at first. I have known several first class

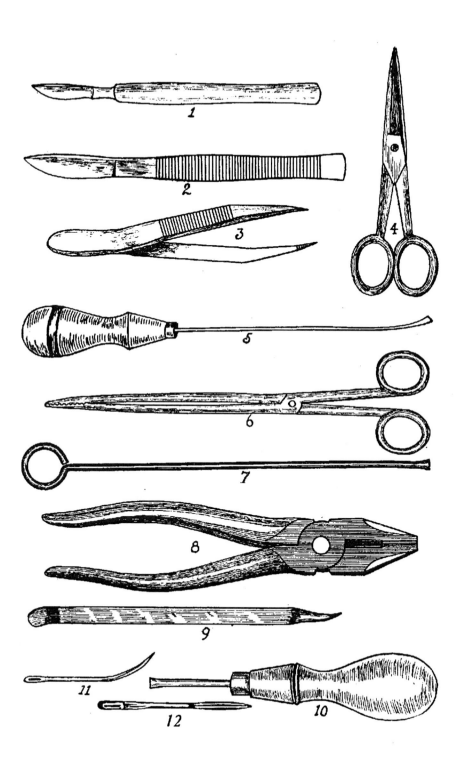

workmen who could make a really fine job of a bird with nothing more than a jack-knife, a pair of scissors, pliers and an old file. While this may be sufficient for one who is a master of his profession, it will pay the beginner to get a few good tools. By this I do not mean one of the elaborate sets sold by some firms, many of the articles in which are either of little use or unnecessary.

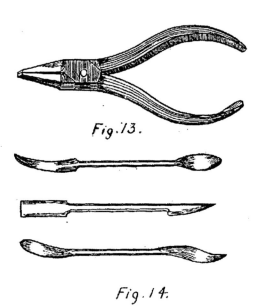

Fig. 13.

Fig. 14.

Our first chapters will deal with the skinning and mounting of birds and small mammals. I will therefore describe the tools which are necessary for this part of the work and leave the others to be described as we proceed.

Most of the articles necessary are described on page 97. Practically all may be purchased from dealers in taxidermist supplies. Nos. 1 and 2 are scalpels used in skinning, No. 3, tweezers for adjusting the feathers of birds and kindred purposes, No. 4, scissors, of which it is better to have two pairs, one fairly heavy for cutting small bones, etc. For the larger birds and mammals a pair of bone snips may be purchased. Nos. 5 and 7 are stuffing irons which the reader can make for himself out of steel wire of various lengths and thicknesses. No. 6 is a pair of stuffing forceps. If desired a blacksmith can fashion these for you out of a pair of old scissors. No. 8, a pair of strong cutting pliers which you will need for cutting wires and for heavy work. No. 9 is a very handy tool and is called a scraper, it can be used to clean the bones and skulls of specimens, to insert eyes and for a multitude of other uses. A blacksmith can easily make one or it may be purchased direct from the dealer. No. 10, an ordinary brad-awl of which two or three sizes had better be secured. No. 11 is a three-cornered needle, known as a surgical needle, and No. 12, a three-cornered straight, or glover's needle. It is better to have a small assortment of these. Fig. 13 is a pair of fine flat-nosed pliers which are indispensable for use on small birds and mammals. Fig. 14 shows three modelling tools of various shapes. The reader can make any number of these from pieces of hard wire or ordinary nails of various sizes and lengths from 3 inches to 7 inches. The ends are heated and then hammered and bent into the shape desired and afterwards finished with a file and grindstone. It is better to temper the metal by plunging it into cold water whilst still hot. Larger modelling tools can usually be purchased at a good hardware store, but they are too large for fine work. You will also require a steel comb to comb out fur and a file to sharpen wires and metal parts.

I am taking it for granted that the reader is possessed of such carpenters' tools as a saw, hammer, brace and bits, and plane. These are indispensable. The student will also require a few artist's sable brushes, and also brushes suitable for varnish, stain, glue and paste. He will need also a feather duster or goose wing to dust out feathers when cleaning birds. The following list of materials will be required for the successful mounting of birds and small mammals. Some fine tow, excelsior, cotton batting, cotton twine and spools of thread, ordinary pins, large and small, very fine cotton or cotton caps for binding the plumage of birds, hardwood sawdust and corn meal, common plaster of Paris, gasoline, artificial eyes, a quantity of glue and coarse building paper for making papier-mache, some ordinary flour, arsenical paste, and corrosive solution. The following artist tube colors (oil), are also needed: Ivory black, Vandyke brown, Flake white, Chrome yellow, Yellow ochre, Prussian blue, Permanent blue, Purple lake, Vermilion, Light red. A greater assortment may be kept if desired but these will suffice for all ordinary purposes.

SKINNING SMALL MAMMALS

The methods given in this lesson will apply to all mammals up to the size of a wolf, with very few exceptions and alterations which will be noted later. We will take for an example that easily-procured and often too common little animal, the Gopher.

Having everything nicely cleared for action place before you on the bench a pot of arsenical paste, Formula (1) and a bottle of corrosive solution, Formula (2).* The small Scalpel, Fig. 1, and

* Before commencing to use any Formula which contains poison see that any sores, cuts or abrasions on the hands are covered with court plaster, and read carefully the notes on poisonous preservatives on last page in book.

the Scissors, Fig. 4, are the only tools required. You will also require a small box (a cigar box will do) containing hardwood sawdust or corn meal, for absorbing the blood and fluids which would make mess of the fur and cause you a lot of unnecessary cleaning if not attended to. Proceed to take careful note of the eyes and any other feature that may help you in the mounting of the specimen. With the scalpel make the opening incision from the center of the abdomen to the vent, taking care that the inner skin which holds the entrails in place is not cut. Now with care, and by pressure with the fingers and an occasional use of the scalpel, separate the skin from the flesh until you reach the place where the hind legs join the body. These must be severed close to the point. By careful skinning you reach the root of the tail. Sever this also close to the body. The skin will now come away easily until you reach the fore legs. These are cut off close to the shoulder blade. Fig. 15, will show you the position and place to cut. Proceed until you reach the ears. These must be cut off quite close to the skull. It is better to cut these well into the ear cavity, for if they are cut off too short it will leave an opening which will spoil the appearance of your specimen when it is mounted.

You next reach the eyes. Cut very carefully the skin which holds the lids around the sockets, be very careful not to cut the eyelids. Next you arrive at the lips. Cut these away close to the skull, being sure to leave the inner skin or gum attached to the skin. Leave the skin attached at the skull at the top of the under jaw and nose. (See Fig. 15).

During these processes be careful not to pull and stretch the skin unduly.

The head is now severed from the body at the base of the skull and l e g s a r e s k i n n e d back right down to the toes, and the flesh cut and scraped from the bones. An opening is made in the base of the skull and the brains removed. The eyes are taken out and the skull t h o r - o u g h l y scraped and cleaned. The root of the tail is skinned with the

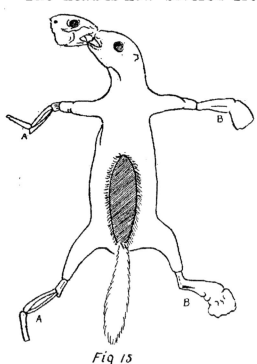

Fig 15

scalpel, and, by placing the fingers around the skin the tail is easily pulled out from its sheath with a pair of pincers. For larger animals two pieces of stick with a notch in each are used. They are placed together over the root of the tail which is then drawn out by main force. During all these process liberal use has been made of sawdust or cornmeal to keep your fingers and the specimen clean. Fig. 15 shows the appearance of the skin just before completion, AA showing the leg bones cleaned of flesh, and BB with the flesh still attached. All particles of flesh and fat that adhere to the skin must now be removed. The skin is now turned right side out and examined, to see if it is soiled by blood or other matter. We will presume that this is the case and proceed as follows:

To Clean a Mammal Skin

With a wad of cotton and a bowl of cold water proceed to clean off all stains from the hair. When this is completed wipe off as much of the surplus water as possible. Next take another wad of cotton saturated in gasoline and apply to the parts previously cleaned. This kills the action of the water and keeps the fur from matting. Now spread the skin on a piece of clean wrapping paper and rub in fine sawdust or corn meal; continue with this until the fur is thoroughly cleaned. When almost dried out it must be combed and beaten in the open air to remove particles of sawdust and other adhering foreign matter. White skins, such as Weasel, are cleaned in the same manner, with the exception that dry plaster of Paris and flour in equal parts is used instead of sawdust. In using sawdust be sure that it is hardwood, otherwise the resin contained in softwood will stick up the fur.

Mounting

The skin being now thoroughly cleaned it is now turned inside out and the skull and leg bones painted with corrosive solution and the skin with arsenical paste.

Next cut six wires, one for the body, four for the legs and one for the tail, each should be at least six inches longer than the part they are for. For an animal of this size 16 or 18 gauge will do. All wires used in mounting must be soft annealed or galvanized iron,* that which is used for stove-pipes will do very well in this case. A very good plan to straighten wires is to fasten one end to something solid, and with the pliers (Fig. 8), pull until all the kinks are out. It is then a simple matter to cut off the lengths desired. The four leg wires are filed to a point at one end and the body and tail wires are sharpened at both ends. They are then sandpapered lightly to allow them to run easily. Now

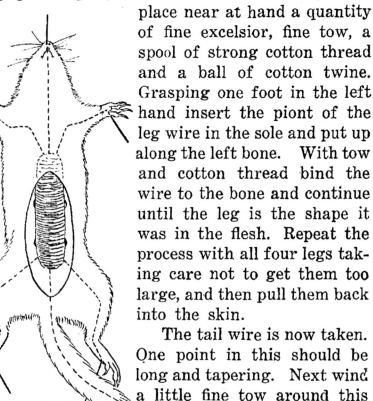

place near at hand a quantity of fine excelsior, fine tow, a spool of strong cotton thread and a ball of cotton twine. Grasping one foot in the left hand insert the piont of the leg wire in the sole and put up along the left bone. With tow and cotton thread bind the wire to the bone and continue until the leg is the shape it was in the flesh. Repeat the process with all four legs taking care not to get them too large, and then pull them back into the skin.

The tail wire is now taken. One point in this should be long and tapering. Next wind a little fine tow around this wire until it is the shape of

Fig. 16

* To anneal wire. Place wire in fire until red hot and then allow to cool slowly. Smooth with sandpaper or emery cloth.

the original tail. The end of the wire that is too fine to cover may be dipped in shellac to prevent it from rusting in the tail sheath. The artificial tail must then be painted with arsenical soap and inserted. Next make a hard body of excelsior bound with twine, much smaller than the original, and push the point of the body wire through this and clinch. The other point of this wire is then pushed through the brain cavity and out through one of the nostrils. In Fig. 18 is seen the method by which the wires are fastened in the false body; AA is the body, BB the tail, CC the right fore leg and DD the left hindleg. The two wires have been omitted so as not to confuse the reader with too many lines. They are of course fastened in the same manner. Fig. 16 shows position of wires and false body inside the skin.

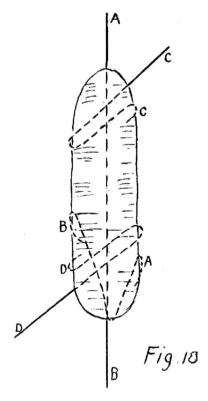

Fig. 18

The next step is to chop up some tow fine with scissors.* Having before you the stuffing rod (Fig. 5), and the forceps (Fig. 6), proceed to fill out the body, commencing at the head, having filled and shaped as far as the shoulders to your satisfaction, place

---

*Where tow cannot be secured, oakum such as is used by plumbers and steam-fitters will do.

a layer of chopped tow along the back between the body and the skin. Next pay attention to the hind quarters and work gradually to the middle. Now with a fine needle (Glover's) commence to sew up the opening in the abdomen, filling and shaping the animal as you proceed. Do not on any account

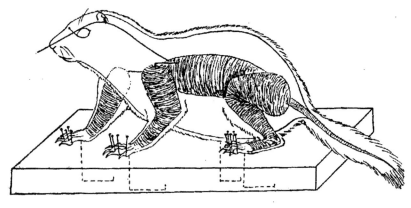

Fig. 17

allow any particles of cotton batting to get mixed with the tow as it is impossible to get a smooth finish with this material. You may also wish to drive a pin or sharpened wire into the specimen to hold some particular part in place, this also may be impossible with cotton.

DETERMINING THE POSTURE

We will presume that the gopher is now nicely filled, and that every attention has been paid to the modelling with the tow of the various features. You have decided to place it in a running position. A small block of wood (1 inch board) is secured as a temporary stand and four holes are drilled in it with the awl (Fig. 10), in the position that the animal would occupy in life. Fig. 17 shows the gopher in outline with the position of the limbs and false body indicated. The dotted lines show the position of the wires in the board, a groove being cut underneath and the wire clinched and fastened with small stables.

The animal being now roughly in position we will proceed to finish the head. With some tow chopped very fine, fill in the cheeks, etc., see also that the place where the skull joins in the neck is also nicely modelled, be careful not to overdo this. Next, with papier-mache, proceed to model the lips and fill the eye sockets. Then insert a pair of glass eyes of the correct size and color. Be sure that both sides of the face are in proportion and the eyes exactly opposite each other, and that the lids, nostrils, lips and all other facial structures are nicely modelled in shape. The scraper (Fig. 9) is very useful for this, also the modelling tools shown in Fig. 14. The corners of the eyes may be held in place with fine entomological pins as shown. Now proceed to put the ears in shape by placing them between two very small pieces of thin pasteboard and holding them in place with pins. The rest of the body is now shaped by a little pressure here and there with the fingers. It may also be necessary to give a little more fullness in places, this may be done by pushing a sharp needle through the skin and lifting the filling where necessary. Now with an old tooth brush attend to the hair, but do not flatten it down. Lastly pin the toes in their correct places and place the specimen to one side to dry. It is best to take a look at it once in a while to see that it is drying in good shape.

The preceding instructions are sufficient for all small mammals up to the size of a rabbit. Animals larger than that and up to the size of a wolf are treated in the same manner with the following alterations and additions. After the legs have been skinned down, there still remains the pad, or sole of the foot which is difficult to turn. It is therefore better to open these from underneath, and remove the fat and flesh which is found there. Always be sure to skin the toes right down to the claws, do not cut the attachment. Next pare down the pads until only the tough skin is left. In opening the pad do not split it down the middle but make the cut at one side. The advantage of this would be readily seen if the animal were to be mounted in such a position that one or more of the pads were seen as is often the case. In such animals as the beaver, otter, and wolf, the tail must be split underneath and skinned right out to the tip.

After being skinned in this manner the hide is lightly salted and left for a day or so rolled up with the hair outside. This is to make the flesh firm. The skin is then placed over a fleshing beam and every particle of fat and flesh removed, as described in the section on Tanning. It is then placed in a pickle, Formula 3, for a few days. During this time it must be frequently turned and looked over to see that the pickle penetrates every place. If this is not attended to the skin may remain in folds in places and the hair come out. The skull should be thoroughly cleaned in the meantime by boiling and scraping while hot. Bear in mind that too much boiling will cause the teeth to fall out.*

The hide is taken from the pickle and hung up to drain. It is then washed out quickly in clear water and drained again. Next place it over the beam and squeeze out all the surplus moisture with the knife (Fig. 4, Tanning). Next insert the wires in the legs and bind them to the bones in the manner previously described. Insert the false tail, and if it has been opened underneath, sew it up, previously painting it with arsenical paste. Next paint the skin all over on the inside with the paste.

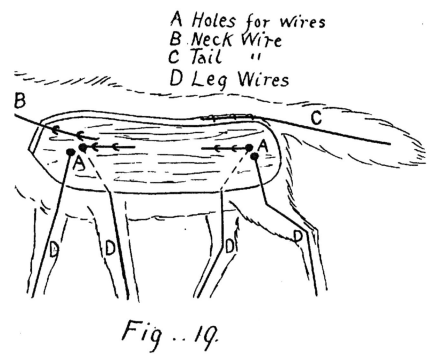

A Holes for wires
B Neck Wire
C Tail "
D Leg Wires

Fig .. 19.

In place of the false body used in the smaller animals, cut out a piece of 1 inch board as shown in Fig. 19. The end of the neck wire is now bent over and inserted in the brain cavity of the skull and fixed there with plaster of Paris. Four holes are now drilled in the board as shown at AA and the leg wires are passed through and stapled at the other side in such a manner that they will hold the animal perfectly rigid. It is very essential that all wires should be fixed firmly otherwise you will have great difficulty in getting the specimen to stay in proper position. Be careful also to use only annealed wire.

The neck and tail wires are now stapled into place and the body filled with fine excelsior in place of the tow in the smaller animals. Tow may, of course, be used where necessary. Should you desire to have the animal with the mouth open, snarl-, ing, fighting, etc., follow the directions given in Rug Making. A careful study of the habits and peculiarities of expression of the subject in hand is essential. The fur must be thoroughly combed and brushed out, and left as nearly in a state of nature as possible. Collect all the good drawings and photographs of animals that you can, but above all get in touch with nature and study the creatures in their natural haunts. Do not be discouraged with failure nor satisfied with partial success.

SKINNING AND STUFFING BIRDS

By a peculiar coincidence, just as I was about to go out and secure a specimen for use in this lesson, a sharp shinned hawk, forgetting that its meal ticket had expired, saw fit to attack one of my chickens. I immediately decided to make an example of it in more ways than one. Being a fairly tough customer in every respect he will answer very well for our lesson, the mode of procedure being the same in all birds, with few exceptions and alterations which will be noted later. Laying the bird before you on the bench on its back proceed to fill the nostrils, mouth, vent, and any shot holes there may be with cotton batting. This is to pre-

vent the blood and secretions from escaping and mussing up the feathers. This accomplished, proceed to spread the feathers and make the opening incision from the middle of the breast bone to the vent, taking care that the inner skin that holds the entrails in place is not cut. Have handy a quantity of cornmeal, which apply liberally as you proceed with the skinning, to absorb the fluids and keep the feathers and keep your fingers clean.

We find now that the wings are in the way and interfere with the proper handling of the bird. Lay the bone of the wing across the corner of the bench and quite close to the body strike it a sharp blow with a small hammer. This gives a clean break and allows the wing to be moved with facility. Repeat this with the other wing.

Fig 20.

Proceed to separate the skin from the flesh until you reach the legs which sever at the second joint from the body. (Fig. 20, C shows the place). Next skin carefully around the vent and sever the tail at the root, but not so close as to cut the roots of the feathers. This will allow you to skin down the back. Now double and tie a piece of twine and loop this around the thighs as shown in Fig. 20 A. Hang the bird to the ceiling by this string and have it at a convenient height so that it can be skinned readily. Having the bird suspended you now have both hands at liberty. Proceed by careful skinning with the fingers and scalpel until you reach the butts of the wings, sever these at the place where they were previously broken, and proceed to skin down the neck until the base of the skull is reached.

Where Details Count

It is better at this stage to lay the bird on the bench, as if it is hung up too long it is apt to stretch the skin unduly. By careful skinning you reach the ears. Dig these out from the cavity of the bone in which they set and continue until you reach the eyes. Great care must be used here so that you do not cut the lids or the eye and let out the fluids. Continue until you reach the base of the beak and be very careful not to sever the skin here. It must be left attached. Now sever the head from the body by cutting off a very small portion of the base of the skull (Fig. 21 A). Remove the eyes from the sockets, being careful not to cut away the bony projection which is seen just above the eye. This projection is peculiar to birds of this class and if removed it will not be possible for you to give to the specimen the keen expression characteristic of the birds of prey.

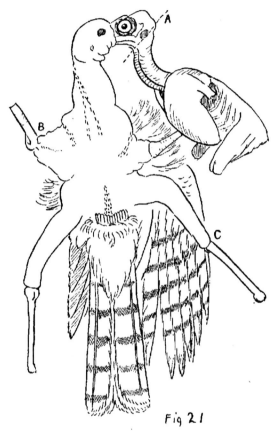

Fig 21

By cutting away a little more of the base of the skull and palate remove the brains and scrape away all surplus flesh from the skull. Next skin down the wings as far as the next joint B and remove the flesh. Now turn your attention to the legs and treat them in a like manner, skinning them just below the joint C. Proceed now to clean away the flesh and soft tissues from the root of the tail. At the extreme end of the backbone and above the tail are two fatty glands, the secretion in which is very oily and is used by the bird to dress its feathers. These must be removed. Be careful not to injure the roots of the feathers or they will come out. Scrape away any particles of flesh or fat that adhere to the skin and anoint the legs and wing bones, skull, and root of the tail with corrosive solution.

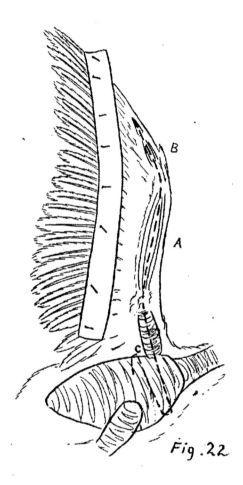

Fig. 22

Now with fine tow and cotton thread bind the leg and wing bones to the exact shape they were before the flesh was removed. Next cure the skin by the application of arsenical paste. Put a little chopped tow in the skull and turn the skin the right side out. Make an incision in the soles of the feet and with a hooked and pointed wire draw out the tendons and s e v e r them.

The flesh still remains in the second portion o fthe wings (Fig. 22A). To remove make an incision underneath, and skin, scraping the bone thoroughly. Two fold of skin are now found to be together at the outer edge of the wing. These must be carefully parted until the extreme outer edge is reached. Here you will find a strong tendon which must be removed. There is also a small piece of flesh in the last joint of the wings (Fig. 22, B) which must be removed from underneath. Paint all places with corrosive solution.

If the feathers are a little soiled they may be cleaned after the bird is wired and filled. But if it is badly soiled, as it will be if you have failed to stop the nostril beak the other channels of escaping fluid, you must proceed to clean it now in the following manner: with cold water and a wad of cotton batting, clean off all blood and tissue repeatedly changing the water in bad cases. When all is removed sponge out all the surplus water. Take another wad of cotton and apply gasoline to the wet portions. It will not do any harm if you wipe over the whole bird with this as it will remove any grease that may have come in contact with the feathers.

Lay the bird now on a clean sheet of wrapping paper and apply a quantity of plaster of Paris, working it into the feathers until they are almost dry, and then beating out the surplus in the open air, using the goose wing for this. A very good thing to fluff out the feathers with is an old-fashioned bellows.

Where there is a lot of cleaning to do, it is better to do it before you apply the poison to the skin, afterward turning the bird inside out and applying the poison as described previously. Small birds can be cleaned very well by placing them in a box with plaster and shaking it thoroughly until all the feathers are cleaned, the water and gasoline being applied first, of course. Birds with glossy or bright-colored plumage are best cleaned with corn meal or hot silver-sand used in the same manner as the plaster. The bird being thoroughly cleaned is ready for mounting.

MOUNTING BIRDS

First make a hard body a little smaller than the original* of fine excelsior bound with cotton twine. Cut three wires, two for the legs, and one for the body and neck. For a bird of this size about six inches longer than the parts for which they are intended and about 16 gauge will be required. Be sure that it is annealed. With a file sharpen the leg wire at one end and the the body wire at both. Push the body wire through the false body, bend over one end and push this through also and clinch it. (Fig. 23, A). With tow bind a false

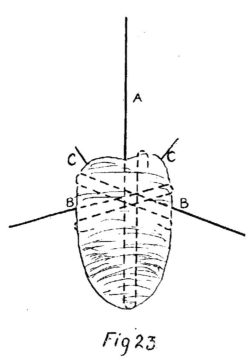

Fig 23.

neck over the wire A, having it a little shorter than the original. Now insert the sharpened end of the leg wire in the sole of th 'foot, and push it up the back of the leg, behind the first joint and up through the tow with which you bound the leg. Repeat this

---

* It is a good plan to lay the original body on the bench before you and take measurements with a pair of calipers, making the false body a little smaller than these measurements.

with the other leg. Now carefully insert the neck wire inside the skin and push it through the skull, continuing until the false neck is in its right place. This done, grasp the leg wire with the right hand, and insert it in the body well up toward the shoulder (B. B. Fig 23). The reason for this is that one part of the leg has been dispensed with, as will be seen by referring to Fig. 20 C, and the wires are inserted where that joint would occur with the bird in a natural position. Be careful of this, as it is a common error to get these wires too low, and if this is the case you will not be able to balance your bird properly. The wires are pushed through, returned, and clinched as shown in Fig. 23.

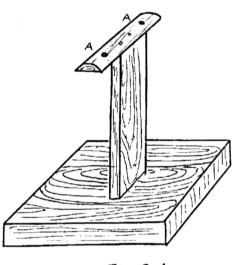

Fig. 24.

Cut up some tow fine and proceed to fill in the space between the body and skin, paying particular attention to the set of the shoulders and tail. Do not fill too much or you will have great difficulty afterwards in getting the feathers to lay in their proper place. Now with a needle and thread, commencing at breast, proceed to sew up the incisions taking care not to gather in the feathers. If you have not done so the bird is now cleaned by the process given previously.

Proceed now to make a temporary perch by taking a piece of board 6 inches square, and nailing a T piece to this. Next drill two small holes to receive the leg wires. Fig. 24. Now cut a number of small wires about four inches long and sharpen them at one end. Insert one into the root of the tail and put into the body to hold the tail in place. Now bend the neck and legs roughly into shape, and set it on the perch by placing the leg wires through the two holes (A. A. Fig. 24) fastening with small staples underneath. Give the bird the pose you wish to assume by bending the neck and legs into shape.

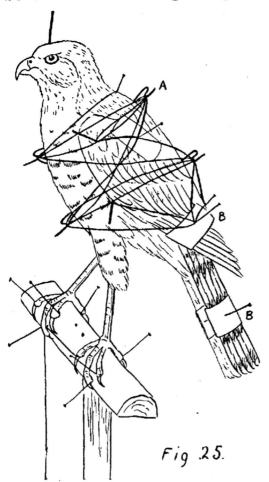

Fig. 25.

The wings now need attention. Take the one nearest you and hold it temporarily in place. Note the set of the shoulders and see if it requires more filing here. This will likely be the case. Make a small incision in the skin underneath the wing and with a small rod or the stuffing forceps, place a little chopped tow where it is needed. Now pin the wing into place with two of the sharpened wires and repeat the process with the other wing. See that the wing coverts lay nicely and naturally in place.

The head n o w claims attention. From the beak and eyes fill in chopped tow until it is the correct shape, commencing w h e r e the neck joins the skull. When completed pass a fine needle and thread through the nostrils and tie the b e a k together. Now insert the eyes, t h e color and size of which you have previously noted. First fill the orbit with a little f i n e papier-mache or potter's clay then

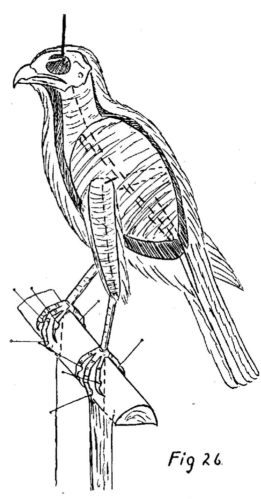

Fig 26.

set the eyes and draw the lids nicely into shape. Do not have the eyes protruding, especially in birds of this class. It is here you will see the value of leaving attached the bony ridge above the eye as, without it you could never give the bird that fierce and keen expression, that is so characteristic of it. Be sure that both eyes are set exactly alike.

Look the bird over and see that its position is correct. Take four more wires pointed at one end and bend them into the shape indicated in Fig. 25, A. Push these into the body as shown, and then proceed with the tweezers to put every feather in its proper place. To do this properly will take some time. It is however, one of the most important parts of the work. The wings and tail are held in shape between strips of pasteboard held together by pins (B. Fig. 25). The bird is then bound with very fine cotton or cotton caps* to hold the feathers in place during the process of drying, and the feet pinned into their proper shape. Much depends upon the care and attention given to these details. Fig. 25 shows the bird in position upon the temporary stand, smoothed, bound and pinned into shape. Fig. 26 is the same bird with one side removed, as it were, to show the position of the false body, legs, wires, etc., the shaded portion represents approximately the amount and position of the loose filling of chopped tow.

SKINNING HEADS OF BIRDS

Such birds as ducks, woodpeckers, cranes, and herons, have heads too large to allow them to pass readily through the neck. In this case the neck is severed as close to the skull as possible inside, and the skin turned right side out. The head is

---

* Cotton caps are spools of very soft cotton thread and are used in the factories for the weaving of cotton cloth. They may be obtained from a dealer in Taxidermist supplies.

then skinned out from a cut in the back of the neck as shown in Fig. 27. This incision is sewn up during the process of mounting with a very fine needle and thread, taking care not to gather in the feathers.

REMOVING FAT FROM SKINS OF BIRDS

Many birds, especially ducks, have a thick layer of fat inside the skin. This must in all cases be removed before you attempt to cure or mount the bird. I have tried many processes but finally came back to carefully cutting away the fat with a sharp pair of scissors, and then scraping the surplus away with a dull knife, using corn meal or hardwood sawdust liberally to absorb the grease.

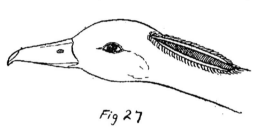

Fig 27

To clean the skin of a very fat duck properly requires more time than it does to skin and mount it. Should the feathers have become at all greasy they should be cleaned by the liberal use of gasoline and sawdust.

MOUNTING BIRDS WITH SPREAD WINGS

Should you wish to mount a bird with its wings spread, flying or fighting, proceed in the same manner as advised previously with the following additions. In place of the three wires for the legs and body, cut five, the two additional ones for the wings. Sharpen these at both ends and have them considerably longer than the full length of the wing bones. Run one end along the various joints to the extreme tip of the wing bone and bind the inside end to the bone reproducing the flesh with tow. Fill in the cavity between the bones at A and B (Fig. 22), with tow and neatly sew up the incisions.

Having inserted the neck wire into the skin and through the skull proceed to push the wing wire through the false body at the point in the shoulder (C. Fig. 22 and 23). Turn it back and clinch it in the manner shown. This may be a little difficult at first, the wire being solid in the wing and having no play whatever. Careful work with the pliers will get it into shape. The dotted line Fig. 22 indicates the position of the wire in the wing and body. Both wings are treated in the same manner. Proceed with the mounting as described before, the only difference being that the wings are braced into shape with pasteboard in the manner shown. Remove it from the temporary stand and fix it to the one it is going to occupy permanently. Color the legs, beak, etc., as described in the section on coloring, first cutting off and removing any projecting wires, taking off the bindings and noting that the feathers lay well in place.

DEAD GAME

Very excellent results may be achieved by mounting ducks, geese, pheasants and other birds as dead game. The birds are skinned in the usual manner and wired, wings, legs and body. In this case the wires are much lighter than would be required to mount a bird of the same size in the ordinary manner. The eyes are left either closed or only half open. It is a good plan to first hang the bird upon the wall and pose it in a natural manner, then with a pencil make an outline. This will help you greatly to get the right hang afterward. Dead game look very well in the cases described in the section on making paper forms. The usual method is to mount the birds upon a wooden panel.

SKINNING AND MOUNTING A HORNED HEAD

In this case we will take as an example the head of a deer. We have selected a specimen with the neck skin cut off well down to the shoulders and brisket, and not damaged or cut up in any way. Lay the head before you on the bench in the position shown in Fig.28. The opening cuts are made as indicated one straight down the back of the neck to a point directly behind the horns A. A. and two others to the center of the base of the horns

Fig. 28.

A. B. Proceed with the point of the knife to loosen the hide around the horns cutting upward and being careful that the skin comes away clean. When the horns are freed at the top, proceed to sever the ears from the skull.

By careful skinning complete the work on the horns and continue until you reach the eyes. Great care must be exercised here so that the eyelids are not cut. Directly in front of the eye is a wax duct which must be dug out with great care from the cavity of bone in which it sets. In working about the mouth be sure and leave at least an inch of the inner skin or gum attached to the hide. If this is not done it will not be possible to model the face properly. Proceeding carefully you come to the nostrils which must be cut away in the same manner as the lips.

The skin is now entirely detached from the skull. By careful cutting and pressure with the fingers 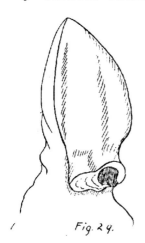 separate the outer skin of the ears from the cartilage until the ear is entirely inverted (Fig. 29). Be careful when you reach the edges that the skin does not tear away as this is a difficult place to mend properly. The inner and outer skin of the nostrils and lips must now be separated but on no account must the inner skin be cut away. Next carefully salt every part of the flesh side of the head skin, or scalp, as it is called and roll up, hair side out, for a few days.

Fig. 29.

The next job is to remove all the flesh from the skull. Professional taxidermists as a rule use a mallet and chisel. This is not so difficult as it would seem, for once the different points are learned the flesh can be cleaned off in half an hour, the secret being to commence at the point of the lower jaw and the nose and get the chisel between the flesh and the bone and continue in this manner. Do not try to move the flesh by cutting away small pieces.

Perhaps an easier way for the amateur is to boil

the head being careful not to overdo the process, and to remove the flesh whilst it is still very hot. A piece about 2 inches wide is then cut out of the base of the skull and the brain removed. After every particle of flesh is removed the skull is painted over with arsenical solution Formula 12, and left to dry. Be sure to clean the skull thoroughly or your job will eventually be infested with insect pests.

After the scalp has laid in salt for a couple of days, proceed to remove all the surplus flesh with the currier's knife. The skin being placed on the fleshing beam for this purpose. I have found that the adjustable draw-knife is best to work around the nose and lips. During this process be very careful not to make any cuts in the skin. If you are unlucky enough to make a couple of gashes keep smiling, they can be mended. When the scalp is properly fleshed it should be washed out in clean water and then hung up to drain. It is then placed in the pickle (formula 3), for several days and thoroughly stirred and turned each day, to insure the pickle penetrating every portion.

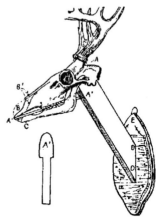

Fig. 30.

The next step in the process is to get the head in shape. With a hand drill if you have one or a brace and ⅛ inch drill, make four holes around each horn in the position indicated by A, Fig. 30. These holes should not be more than ⅜ inch deep and should then be filled with small wooden plugs cut off level with the bone. These plugs should then be marked with black paint or indelible pencil. The purpose of these plugs is to afford a means of nailing the skin tightly around the horns, when the head is mounted, and they are marked so that they may be easily seen. Next drill two small holes through the skull into the brain cavity. Now cut a piece of 2x2 lumber about 18 inches long and fit one end into the brain cavity, and fix it there at right angles to the top of the skull by driving nails into it through the two holes you have just drilled. Make sure that the neck-piece is in proper alignment with the skull. Now mix a quantity of plaster of Paris, fill in the brain cavity around the neck piece and leave to harden. Now cut out a piece of wood to fit in the nose as shown in B. Don't have this too large or it will interfere with subsequent modelling. The next thing required is a lip piece, made of soft ½ inch pine and the shape shown in A. When the plaster is thoroughly set around the neck piece fix the piece in the nose by drilling small holes as indicated by B and nailing. The lip piece is now fitted into position AA and nailed to the nose and neck pieces. Now drill a hole through the jaw at C and fix with a wood screw.

The next thing is to cut off the neck piece to the correct length and angle. The length of course depends a great deal on the scalp. We will presume this is ample. Have some one hold up the head with the neck-piece against a door-jamb or post, and retire some distance to get a proper view of the head. When you get it to suit mark the neck piece with a pencil as indicated by D. D. and saw it off.

From a piece of ⅞ inch board cut a neck-board. The shape of this will vary considerably according to the length of neck. If it is cut well down to the shoulders it will be about the shape shown in Fig. 31, 1. Just above the shoulders it will resemble 2, and shorter 3, getting almost circular just behind

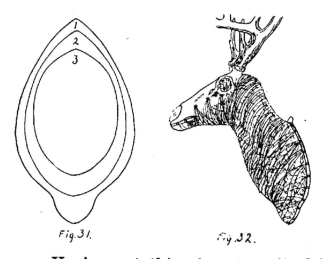

Fig. 31.   Fig. 32.

the ears. Having cut this piece to suit, drill two holes obliquely through the back of the board and bend a wire as shown at Fig. 30 E. This should be firmly stapled on the inside, and is to hang up the head during the process of mounting. This done, fix the board to the neck-piece with screws from the back. Be sure that the board is properly centered and not over to one side. The neck board must then be countered by nailing pieces across the grain as shown to prevent it warping, Fig. 32 shows the next step. Nails are driven partially in as shown around the neck board lip-piece and on the sides of the face, and the neck and face are built up with fine excelsior and string. The excelsior will make a tighter and smoother job if dampened with water. A little plaster of Paris is now put into the eye-sockets. Keep this well back so as to allow plenty of room for modelling material. The head is now placed to one side. Be sure that it is correct and smooth, as no filling is permissible.

PREPARING THE SCALP

Remove the scalp from the pickle and allow it to drain. Give it a good washing in clean water and drain again. Place it over the fleshing beam and squeeze out all the surplus moisture by working the flesh side with currier's knife. See that the eyes, lips, nostrils, etc., are in good shape, and proceed to sew up all shot holes and cuts that you may have made.* Those in the neck are sewn with Barbour's linen thread or Gilling twine coated with shoemaker's wax. It will be necessary to use four or six ply of this according to the thickness of the skin. The shoemaker's wax may be coated with soap to make it slip more easily in the wet skin. The small cuts on the face must be sewn with strong linen thread. Three cornered needles are always used.

The next thing is to cut two pieces of pliable paste-board the size and shape of the ears and coat them with shellac or hot paraffin. These are inserted behind the cartilage and held in place by stitches. These must be nicely hidden and the hair combed over them. Some taxidermists advise taking out the cartilage altogether, but I find by expe-

---

* Barbourous linen thread or gilling twine known as shoemaker's thread, is found to be the best for sewing up heads, etc.

rience that the ears have a tendency to split after the head has been mounted a year or two. This is due to the dry heat to which most heads are subjected, hung high on walls in rooms which are closed tight for six months in the year. For the same reason it is better not to thin down the lips and nose too much. The ears having been attended to, the scalp is now brushed over with Arsenical soap on the inside, and placed over the skull and neck, or manikin as it is now called. Adjust the eyes by driving a small nail into the wax duct and nail the skin in proper place around the horns by driving small nails into the plugs which were previously placed there and marked. Next tack the skin temporarily to the center of the neckboard and commencing at the horns proceed to sew up the cuts in the back with a large three-cornered needle and strong thread. After you have sewn a little way down the neck fill in the butts of the ears with excelsior and then proceed to finish the sewing. During this process be careful that the neck does not rest on the corner of the bench. Should it do so it will likely leave a dent in the manikin that will show when the head is dry. Now trim off the surplus skin around the neck board and fasten with shingle nails about one inch apart.

Having mixed a quantity of papier-mache, commence at the lower lip and shape nicely. A very little chopped tow can be used at the back of the mouth and cheeks if necessary. Now tack the lip to the lip-piece and proceed to model the nose and lips. The inner skin which has been left on, forms a bag. Place a roll of composition in this and model the lips into shape. Use a modelling tool for filling, etc., but the most of the shaping is better done with the fingers and thumb, using both hands together and standing directly in front of the head. By this means you are more likely to get both sides alike.

Next come the eyes. Fill in around the wax duct with papier-mache and be sure that it is properly closed and correctly shaped. Having the eyelids in fair shape and both sides alike, insert the eyes and nail the corner to the bone with a shingle nail. You probably noticed in skinning the head that the skin was attached closely to the bone at this point. Do not have the eyes too staring. A deer as a rule has a quiet docile expression. Now attend to the ears. Fill the butts nicely to shape with chopped tow.

Cut and sharpen two stout wires. Insert those in the tips of the ears and push them down the back and into the manikin to hold the ears in position. The head is now brushed and combed into shape and hung upon the wall to dry, during which process it should have careful attention.

FINISHING THE HEAD

When thoroughly dry, take down the head and cut off the nails around the horns and remove the wires from the ears. Brush the head thoroughly until perfectly clean and wash the horns to remove any stains or dirt that may be upon them.

Finish and smooth around the eyes and nostrils with very fine papier-mache which may be colored with brown umber. Allow this to dry. Then paint these places with a mixture of Vandyke brown and lamp black (artist's colors) mixed with turpentine. The bare skin of the nose may also be touched lightly with it. Clean the eyes with a little turpentine on a small piece of rag and polish them. Next brush the horns with a mixture of turpentine and linseed oil in equal parts, and rub off the surplus. This gives them the right amount of life. Never on any account varnish horns.

The next consideration is a shield on which to fasten the head. If you are handy with carpenters' tools you can no doubt make one, otherwise you can have one especially made, or order one from the dealer in taxidermy supplies. They are made in a variety of shapes and designs the one most commonly used being an oval with a moulded edge. This fits the head fairly well. For many years I made a pattern in the way shown in Fig. 33. Place the neck on a large piece of wrapping paper and draw a margin around it as shown by the dotted line about 3 inches wide in this case. Next cut out the four semi-circles and you have a pattern that has the advantage of fitting the head and also of being of good design. A pattern can be made for

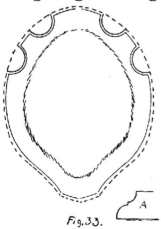

any head by proceeding in the same m a n n e r. This is a great advantage when making a collection of heads that are to be hung in one place. The edge of the shield is usually finished with a mould. The one shown in A is more commonly used but can however be varied to suit.

Fig.33.

This branch of taxidermy is probably the most difficult of all, and the results usually achieved are the most disappointing. The majority of stuffed fish bear very little resemblance to the original in form and practically none at all in color and transparency. To such an extent is this the case that many museums have discarded this method in favor of the more exact and scientific mode of reproduction in plaster, papier-mache, etc. However, the taxidermic method being still in vogue, and many sportsmen still preferring to have the actual fish preserved rather than have a more lifelike cast made of it I will describe the method briefly.

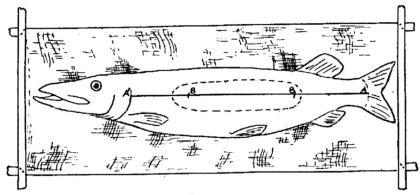

Fig. 34.

We will take for example a jackfish or pike. Making a temporary framework on which tack a piece of fine sacking or strong cotton cloth, Fig. 34, and prop this up some inches from the bench. This stretcher is kept constantly damp, and is better than a board to skin the fish on, in that it conforms more to the shape of the fish and is therefore less liable to damage it.

Next lay the fish on a large piece of wrapping paper, and with a long pencil make a correct outline of it and take notes of its color and peculiarities. This is better explained by Fig. 35, which is a copy

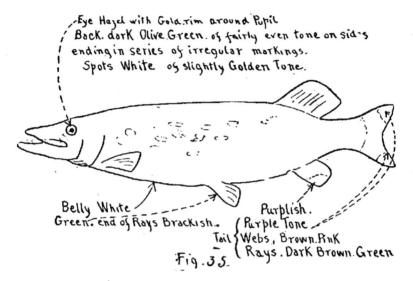

Eye Hazel with Gold rim around Pupil
Back. dark Olive Green. of fairly even tone on sides ending in series of irregular markings.
Spots White of slightly Golden Tone.

Belly White
Green. end of Rays Brackish.
Purplish.
Purple Tone
Tail { Webs, Brown.Pink
Rays. Dark Brown. Green

Fig. 35.

of a chart I made of a jack-fish, and the original notes. This is not a set example but can be varied according to requirements. This accomplished, examine the fish and decide which is the best side. Cover this with thin paper, which will adhere readily to the mucus or slimy covering peculiar to fishes. This precaution is to help the scales to stay in place. Next lay it best side down upon the stretcher, Fig. 34, and proceed with a large pair of scissors or bone snips to cut the scapular arch (this is a large bone just underneath the gill covers) at A.1. Continue with the scissors to make a straight cut the entire length of the body of the fish A1.A.

With a sharp knife separate the skin from the flesh on both sides of the cut, until the fins are reached. These must be cut off on the inside. The skin is usually quite thin in these places, so be careful not to cut it as the skin of a fish is exceedingly hard to repair. The fins and tail severed, continue to skin on the underside. When this is accomplished sever the head from the body at the shoulders, and the body will come away clean. During this work care has been taken not to wrinkle the skin unduly and to keep it moist. Remove all particles of flesh from the base of the fins, tail, etc., an operation requiring great care, and also scrape off any pieces that may have been left attached to the skin.

The head now claims your attention. Cut away a small portion of the base of the skull and remove the brains, also the eyes and the flesh from the

Fig 38

cheeks, and all other cavities. This is quite a job and must be done from the inside. It is best accomplished by a scraper, of which various sizes can be made from pieces of hard wire, old flat files, etc., as shown in Fig. 38. The tongue also must be removed. This requires great care. The skin is now painted on the inside with arsenical paste and is ready for filling.

Proceed to model the head with fine papiermache, and chopped tow, taking care to fill all the places where the flesh has been removed. The body of the fish can be filled with a variety of materials, such as sawdust, sand, bran, dry plaster of Paris, and chopped tow. Personally I prefer a mixture of sawdust and plaster. The skin being laid on the stretcher commence at the head, sewing up the skin and patting it into shape with a flat wooden paddle as you proceed. Having filled about a quarter of the length of the fish, start at the tail which treat in the same manner. During this work have constant reference to your outline sketch, and also pay attention to the fins and tail and see that they are kept damp otherwise they will split. A common error is to get a fish too long. Be careful then to keep it shortened as you proceed.

The whole being nicely filled and patted into shape and sewn as far as B. B. Fig. 34, cut a piece of board the comparative size of which is indicated by the dotted line, and attach two wires as shown in Fig. 37. This is inserted in the fish with the wires protruding and the remainder of the incision sewn up. Next cut a piece of board a little larger than the fish, and drill two holes corresponding to the position of the wires. Attach the board to the fish by passing the wires through the holes and fastening them at the back with staples, and turn the fish right side up.

Carefully remove the paper which has held the scales in place, and pat the fish nicely into shape with a wooden paddle. Should any more filling be required it may be inserted under the gill covers and worked into place with a stuffing rod, which should be made of a piece of flat smooth lath for fish, the ordinary rod being of no use for this kind of filling. Adjust the fins and tail and keep them in shape by placing them between two pieces of pasteboard which are pinned together at the edges. Avoid pinning through the fins if possible.

Now pay attention to the head, see that it is properly adjusted and that the cheeks, jaws and other features are nicely modelled into shape with papier-mache. See that the eyes are also in shape but leave sufficient room in the orbits to allow you to fill in a little composition when you set the eyes later. The gill covers are pinned into shape and the mouth held in place by having sharpened wires driven into the board, close to the jaws but not through them. Should the head be inclined to sag it is propped up underneath with a little tow, etc.

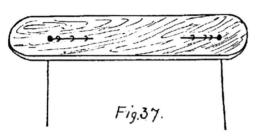

Fig.37.

Fig. 36

The fish is now sponged off clean and given a very thin coat of Damar varnish to keep the scales in place. It is then placed on one side to dry, which will take a month at least. Fig. 36 shows the fish with fins and tail braced and otherwise put into shape for drying.

When thoroughly dry the heavy filling is taken

out, the stitches being opened and the board removed. It is then replaced with chopped tow, or very fine excelsior in the case of large fishes. (In small fish it is not necessary to take out the filling.) The board is replaced and another piece of thin board with the edges bevelled is placed on the back outside the skin, the two being screwed together hold the skin firmly in place.

It is then placed on the panel which it is to occupy permanently, the braces are removed from the fins and tail, and the eyes inserted. These have previously been colored, as mentioned in the chapter on coloring and tinting. Should any of the fins be broken they are mended by sticking pieces of tissue paper on the back with varnish, and the deficiencies in thickness made up with a little hot wax. For final coloring see also chapter on that subject.

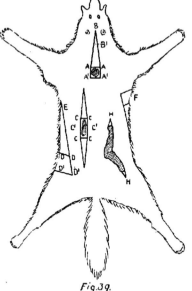

It is advisable when possible to have fish enclosed in a glass case. If you have some artistic ability you can make a very fine duplicate of a fish by following the methods described in Plastering Casting.

Fig.39.

MAKING FUR RUGS AND ROBES

We have before us the skin of a Prairie Wolf, tanned by one of the processes given on tanning.

If you are a beginner you have undoubtedly cut and torn a number of holes in the skin. Do not be discouraged at this as they come from the best professional tanneries or fur dressers in very badly damaged condition at times. Fig. 39 shows the skin laid before you fur side down exposing a number of holes and bad places. Most of these could be fixed by merely sewing in a patch of fur identical in length, color and texture, but as a professional you can take my word that such pieces are hard to find. You may have hundreds of pelts, but you would find that the fur is either too long or short or too light or dark, no two furs being exactly alike. To overcome this difficulty furriers and taxidermists have to make use of what is technically known as a drop. In the shoulder of the skin is seen a round hole, to fix this proceed to cut out the square as shown A.A. A1. A1. (a good sharp knife must be used for this work) and always cut from the skin side, in this way you will not cut any hair. Having removed this square proceed to make two long cuts from A. to B. Now take this triangular piece and with a glover's needle and strong thread sew the points A. A. to the corners A. I. A. I. Continue now to sew in this piece, this will bring B. to

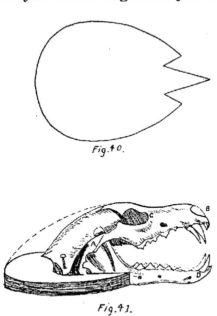

Fig. 40.

Fig. 41.

approximately B.1. The remaining portion is merely sewn together.

We next turn our attention to C.C. C.C. This is too long to allow us to make a single drop so we make a double, bringing the points C.C. C.C. together at C.1. C.1. and proceed as before. In all skins the portions which lie underneath the shoulders and more especially the flanks are almost bare. Although this is perfectly natural it gives the finished rug a somewhat damaged appearance if not attended to. To do this the portion enclosed in D.D., D.1. D.1. is cut out and discarded, and a cut is made from D. to E., and D.D. joined to D.1. D.1., commencing at the inside corner. F. shows a shoulder fixed in a similar manner.

H. H. looks impossible but it is merely a tear which has assumed this appearance and position in the tanning. To fix this moisten the edges with warm water and try and pull it together. It may still fold at the corners, in which case cut out the small triangular pieces as indicated and sew together. During all this work it is presumed that you have constantly examined the fur side to see if the pieces were matching. It sometimes happens that, due to a skin being stale or to improper tanning it is what is known as hair slipped, that is, that the skin is devoid of fur in places. Such places must be cut out and fixed by any of the foregoing methods.

MOUNTING HEADS FOR RUGS

The skin is now nicely repaired and you have decided to have it with a fully mounted head with the mouth open. For our present lesson we will presume you have saved the natural skull.

First immerse the head of the skin in a pail of water to the ears so that it will soften while you proceed with the other work. Next from a piece of soft pine board ⅞ inch thick cut a baseboard as shown in Fig. 40 making the pointed end so that it will fit between the lower jaws, in which you have previously drilled four small holes, two on each side. With nails or small screws fix the lower jaw as shown in Fig. 41. The upper portion is now fixed into position with nails as shown, and held firmly by having the cavities around the hinge of the jaws at A. and the back of the mouth filled with plaster of Paris which has been mixed for the purpose. Several small nails are now driven partially into the edge of the excelsior which is held in place by cotton twine wound back and forth over these nails. The amount of excelsior is indicated by the dotted line and the edge of the board.

Now model a tongue in papier-mache trying to imitate the shape of the natural one as near as possible. Set this away to harden.

Next take the head skin out of the water and wring out all surplus moisture. This done, thin down any places around the nose, lips and eyes that may have been overlooked in the fleshing. Should any of the interior of the lips have been accidentally cut away replace it by sewing on a thin piece of leather. See that the ears are skinned right to the tips and sew up neatly any small holes in the face which you may have cut.

From a piece of pliable pasteboard cut two pieces the shape of the ear cartilages, give these a coat of shellac, or hot paraffin to waterproof them, and insert in the ears. This is to stiffen the ears and prevent them shrivelling. With a fine glover's needle sew the ear through in several places to hold the pasteboard in place. If the under lip has been cut it should now be neatly sewn together. Brush the skin of the head over with arsenical paste, and place it over the skull. A plug of wood has previously been inserted in the nose cavity as shown in Fig. 41 B. With a fine nail fix the center of the inturn of the upper lip to this plug. Next tack the corner of the eyes at C., and fix the lower lip by taking a stitch around the base of the lower incisors at D. See that the butts of the ears and the eyelids are adjusted and then tack the skin around the baseboard.

You are now ready to proceed with the modelling. With some fine papier-mache, model the lips, nose, and other features, into the shape that your previous observations tell you they should assume. To give a snarling effect the lips should be curled back from the teeth and the nose gathered in a series of wrinkles. The main feature is, however, the eyes. Having selected a pair of the right size and color proceed to insert them taking care that they are exactly opposite, and that the lids are properly adjusted. The whole expression may be changed by a slight alteration of the eyelids.

Space forbids me to go into all the details of expression. Proper results can only be gained by experience and constant observation, and I cannot too strongly emphasize the value of taking notes and measurements where possible. Figs. 42, 43 and

44 are merely a reproduction of sketches and measurements of a black bear head which I had for mounting some years ago. They will serve to illustrate my meaning. In addition no opportunity should be lost to make notes from life.

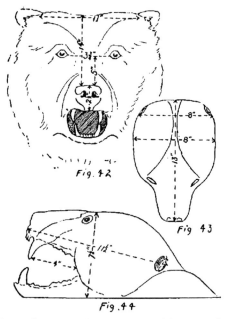

Fig. 42

Fig 43

Fig. 44

The modelling of the features being now completed, the ears should be fixed in position by having a sharpened wire run down the back from the tip and into the excelsior. The fur is now nicely combed into shape and the head placed to one side to dry. In a few days it is taken again and the artificial tongue inserted, and the inside of the mouth, lips and palate modelled and nicely smoothed off with the modelling tools, which are dipped in water, the drying is then repeated.

WAXING AND FINISHING

This next phase of the work should only be undertaken when the head is quite dry.

Prepare a small quantity of wax as described in formula No. 9 and apply quickly whilst hot to the mouth, tongue and surfaces representing membranes with a soft brush (camel hair). Next apply black wax prepared in the same manner, to the lips and nose, and lastly with a little soft modelling wax, formula 10, fill in the eyelids, nostrils, etc., and smooth off with a piece of damp rag. Clean the teeth by scraping off such particles of wax that may have adhered to them and give the mouth a coat of white shellac. The head is now completed and if you have followed the instructions carefully you should be pleased with your job.

STRETCHING THE SKIN

When a skin has been tanned it will not as a rule lay flat therefore it must be stretched. First soak the feet in water for a while and then see that they are nicely pared down. If the fleshing has been properly done in the first place they will be all right. Now with a brush dampen the skin with warm water, taking care to keep the hair dry.

Next stretch the skin on the floor or a board, fur side up with 1½ inch nails about 3 inches apart. Try to get width rather than length, especially in the legs. Pay particular attention to the claws. See that they are properly adjusted and turn down naturally; a little pad of tow placed under the foot will help this. When dry the skin must be taken up and trimmed by taking off the rough uneven edges with a sharp knife. It is now ready for lining.

LINING A RUG

Procure some good felt of the color desired, purchasable from any large dry goods store in widths of six feet. Measure roughly the amount of lineal feet of border that you will require and cut strips 3 inches wide. With a pinking iron proceed to scallop the edge, by placing the felt on a piece of hardwood and striking the iron sharply with a hammer. Pinking irons can be bought from a hardware store or a dealer in taxidermy supplies. Sew the border to the skin. Gather it neatly at the head and feet. Lastly cut out a piece of strong denim or duck, the shape of the skin and a little larger, to allow for the edges being turned in and sew this to the felt border close to the skin. This completes the rug. Should you require it, the rug may be inter-lined with sheet cotton batting; this is advisable where there are seams due to repairing.

HALF HEADS

It is sometimes desired to mount only the upper half of the head on a rug. To do this cut a board the shape as shown in Fig. 45 and place nails around the edge, with fine excelsior and twine, make head similar in shape to Figs. 45 and 46. Proceed as instructed for full heads. This makes a good job and is about one-quarter the work necessary to mount a full head. If the skin is to be lined flat it is only necessary to sew up the eyes, etc., and treat head same as the rest of the skin.

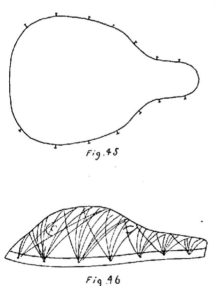

Fig. 45

Fig. 46

The horns of deer, moose, elk, and kindred animals, make very attractive trophies if neatly mounted upon a shield. This class of horns should never be polished or varnished. This must be left as nat-

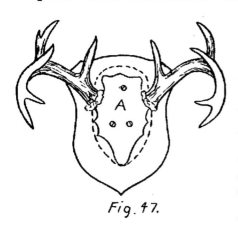

ural as possible by simply washing with warm water and soap and afterwards b r u s h e d over with a mixture of linseed oil and turpentine in equal parts. The surplus is then rubbed off with a piece of rag. This gives just sufficient life to the horns

Fig. 47.

without objectionable gloss. To mount the horns saw off from the skull leaving the frontal bone attached (A. Fig. 47). Next cut out a piece of board as indicated by the dotted line and attach the h o r n s with screws as shown. The bone is now covered with a piece of the natural scalp or with plush or v e l v e t. This i s tacked to the board. The horns are then fixed to a shield, with wood screws from the back.

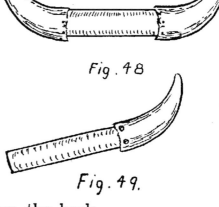

Fig. 48

Fig. 49.

The horns of oxen and buffalo, are as a rule pol-

lop the edge, by placing the felt on a piece of hardwood and striking the iron sharply with a hammer. Pinking irons can be bought from a hardware store or a dealer in taxidermy supplies. Sew the border to the skin. Gather it neatly at the head and feet. Lastly cut out a piece of strong denim or duck, the shape of the skin and a little larger, to allow for the edges being turned in and sew this to the felt border close to the skin. This completes the rug. Should you require it, the rug may be inter-lined with sheet cotton batting; this is advisable where there are seams due to repairing.

HALF HEADS

It is sometimes desired to mount only the upper half of the head on a rug. To do this cut a board the shape as shown in Fig. 45 and place nails around the edge, with fine excelsior and twine, make head similar in shape to Figs. 45 and 46. Proceed as instructed for full heads. This makes a good job and is about one-quarter the work necessary to mount a full head. If the skin is to be lined flat it is only necessary to sew up the eyes, etc., and treat head same as the rest of the skin.

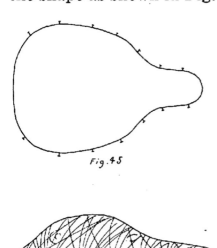

Fig. 45

Fig. 46

The horns of deer, moose, elk, and kindred animals, make very attractive trophies if neatly mounted upon a shield. This class of horns should never be polished or varnished. This must be left as natural as possible by simply washing with warm water and soap and afterwards b r u s h e d over with a mixture of linseed oil and turpentine in equal parts. The surplus is then rubbed off with a piece of rag. This gives just sufficient life to the horns

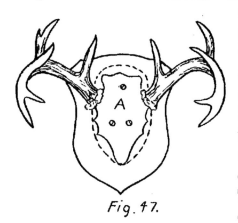

Fig. 47.

without objectionable gloss. To mount the horns saw off from the skull leaving the frontal bone attached (A. Fig. 47). Next cut out a piece of board as indicated by the dotted line and attach the h o r n s with screws as shown. The bone is now covered with a piece of the natural scalp or with plush or v e l v e t. This i s tacked to the board. The horns are then fixed to a shield,

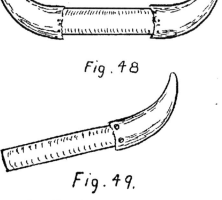

Fig. 48

Fig. 49.

with wood screws from the back.

The horns of oxen and buffalo, are as a rule polished. They must first be removed from the core by boiling; but only boil enough to loosen the horns. Now attach each horn to a stick of wood with screws as in Fig. 49.

Now place the stick in a vise, and if the horn is very rough, as in the case of a buffalo, proceed to pare it down. First work with a draw knife next with a spokeshave, a carpenter's steel scraper or a piece of broken glass, then with fine sandpaper rubbing the way of the grain, and last with a mixture of boiled linseed oil and powdered pumice stone or emery powder, rubbed in with a rag.

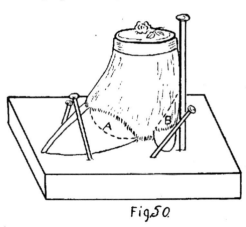

Fig. 50

When polished the horns are taken off the stick, and fixed to the natural skull or to a block of wood as shown in Fig. 48. They may then be fixed to a shield in the same manner as the deer horns.

To Utilize the Hoofs of Big Game

Dealers in taxidermy supplies sell nickel fittings for feet which are in the form of inkwells, jewel cases, thermometers, and bric-a-brac. When the hoofs are nicely polished and fitted with these, they make very attractive ornaments and presents. Fig. 50 shows the foot of an elk in the process of being made into an inkwell or jewel case. The foot is skinned out by being cut down the back and the bone taken out to the last joint, as indicated by the dotted line A. It is then placed in the pickle (Formula 3) for a week or so. When properly tanned it is taken out, washed in cold water and the dew-claws cut off, and sewn on again lower down, as indicated at B. This is so that the hoof will stand. It is then sewn up and filled with chopped tow or excelsior, placed upon a board, and held in place by nails driven around the edge as shown. When dry the hoof is polished with oil and pumice stone, the filling taken out and replaced with plaster of Paris mixed with water. The fitting is put into place while the plaster is wet and the job is complete.

Fig. 51 shows a deer foot mounted with a thermometer. The leg must be left long in this case, and the bone taken out to the last joint. After being cured in the pickle, the bone is replaced by a piece of soft pine cut the same shape,

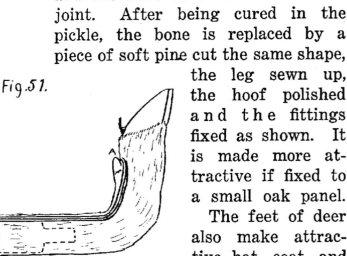

Fig. 51.

Fig. 52.

the leg sewn up, the hoof polished a n d t h e fittings fixed as shown. It is made more attractive if fixed to a small oak panel.

The feet of deer also make attractive hat, coat, and gun racks. Proceed to skin out the leg as before but leave the bone in. After being pickled, two stout wires are inserted as shown in A.A. Fig. 52, and the leg bone is sawn off at B. A block of wood the shape shown in C. is inserted and allowed to project about one inch beyond the skin. The wire is now bound to the bone and papier mache. It is then sewn up and bent into the desired shape. When dry the hoof is polished.

To fix it to a shield or board bore a hole the size of the wood block and make a channel for the wires. The block is inserted in the hole and the wires clinched and stapled at the back.

MAKING ARTIFICIAL HEADS AND ROCKWOOD IN PAPER

The use of paper in making many forms and reproductions used by the taxidermist has of recent years become almost universal.* For the purpose of this lesson we will place before us the cast of a deer h e a d and neck, made in two halves by the process described in casting. The cast having been given several coats of shellac, is then oiled with lard, or a mixture of linseed oil and lard. The material required is ordinary building paper of two colors. Procure that kind which will soften readily in water, some varieties are coated with a resin preparation and are very hard to handle for this purpose.

Fig. 53.

* The uses of papier mache as applied to the art of taxidermy are many. It is used in all places where a modelling composition is necessary in the making of artificial tongues for animals, in modelling the various muscles and fishy parts, in the making of artificial rocks, branches, bark, etc., in reproducing, stone, brick, plaster, stucco, etc., and a thousand and one other things to which the reader can adapt it as he proceeds.

The other requirements are a pot of paste (formula 11) and a good stiff brush is best. Proceed to tear (not cut) the paper into strips about six or eight inches long and two inches wide. Do the same with a quantity of both colors and put them in a pail to soak. When softened squeeze out the surplus water, and, having pasted the strip on both sides proceed to press a layer into the cast, follow with a layer of the other color and repeat until you have six or eight layers in all according to the thickness of the paper.

The reason for the two colors is to indicate when each layer is complete as it is necessary for a good job to have the cast of even thickness throughout. Both sides are treated in the same manner and they are then laid away to dry. This is best done slowly to prevent shrinkage. When dry a piece of board is tacked to the top of the head as shown in Fig. 53 and further secured by having pieces of paper pasted over the joint. This piece provides an attachment for the horns. The two halves are then placed in the cast, and are fastened together by having strips pasted over the joint in the inside. The joint on the outside is then filled with papier-mache, and a board is fixed into the neck as shown in B. The dotted lines indicate that the board is fixed on the inside of the paper form. When dry these forms may be gone over with a coat of hot paraffin to make them waterproof.

In the event of a taxidermist having lots of work in season these forms have the advantage that they can be made up in summer when work is slack. Furthermore they obviate cleaning of the skull, and lastly their extreme lightness and durability is a distinct advantage.

The same process is followed in the making of artificial heads for rugs. Half heads are made in one piece; full heads in two, upper and lower jaw. Sometimes the upper portion is made in two pieces on account of undercuts. These pieces are then fixed together in the same manner as the deer, and the artificial teeth and tongue set in papier-mache. The heads are then finished with wax as recommended in the chapter on rugs.

CASES

Excellent wall cases for birds, etc., can be made in the same manner. The kind I have usually employed have been oval and concave. The method of

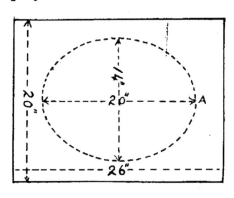

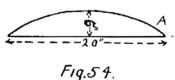

Fig. 54.

making a form for these is as follows: Nail together a board 20 inches by 26 inches (Fig. 54). Then cut out another piece 14 inches by 20 inches and oval in shape, and nail it in position as indicated by the dotted line. Next cut a piece as shown Fig. 54 A. 20 inches by 5 inches and nail it on the center of the oval at A. Then with twine and excelsior make a manikin, first driving nails partly into the edge of the oval piece to hold the twine. This manikin may for convenience be called a convex oval. When completed cover this with a coat of papier-mache and smooth off.

When dry it is coated with shellac and the paper applied as directed for the deer head. Four or five layers will be sufficient for this. When this paper form is dry it can be coated on the inside with kalsomine or alabastine of a grey tone. If you are somewhat of an artist you can then paint an appropriate scenes on this background in oil colors. The

coat of kalsomine causes the paint to assume a dull finish which is preferable for this kind of work. This size of case is suitable for a small duck or grouse. Fig. 57 is a drawing of a case of similar size containing a wood duck, the paper case being inserted in a frame with mat and glass. This is by far the best way of casing birds and small mammals that I know.

Should you be unable to paint the scenery the case will look very well if the background is merely tinted with a light grey or similar unobtrusive tone. The bird is set upon an artificial rock which is made more attractive by the addition of a little moss, grass or other herbage. Some very fine cases may be made with fish in this manner. One of my favorite pieces of work being three small perch, represented in the act of swimming. The background in this case made to represent rocks under water which being of a dark tone set off the brighter colors of the perch to perfection. A dull oak frame is best for these cases and will not detract from the specimen.

To Make Artificial Rock

We will presume you wish to make a rock work stand for a large hawk. Procure a piece of 1 inch board 8 inches square and upon this nail an upright 6 inches high, next nail a cross piece to this and also two pieces to the base to prevent warping.

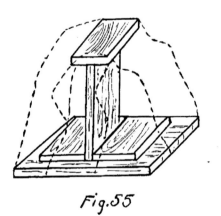

Fig.55

Proceed to tack over this pieces of pasteboard as indicated by the dotted lines in Fig. 55, making them angular. Next cover the whole with strips of paper, pasted as for heads and set away to dry. When dry give the stand a coat of glue and sprinkle on fine sand. Allow this to dry again and color with powder colors and glue size.

Another very good stand made by this process is one that will hang on the wall. This is very good for eagles and other large birds that might otherwise be in the way. To make this, first cut a piece for the back and fix a wire hanger to it (Fig.56). Next fashion a wedge-shaped piece for the front and another for the top. Cover with pasteboard and proceed as before.

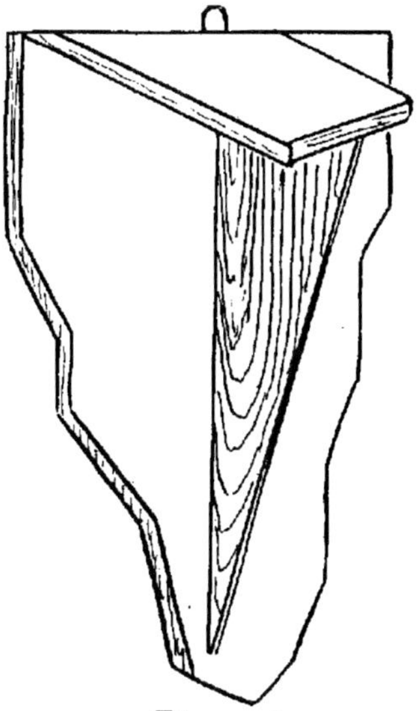

Fig. 56

PLASTER CASTING

A knowledge of plaster casting even in the elementary stages is of great value to the taxidermist of today. By its means he is able to save himself no small amount of labor and in addition he can also achieve better and more artistic results than would otherwise be the case. Plaster of Paris is made in many grades, but for all ordinary purposes of the taxidermist the common variety will suffice. It varies from 3 to 5 cents per pound in quantities.

In handling plaster of Paris it is essential to have everything ready for its application as it sets very quickly when mixed with water. It can be retarded by adding a little glue to the water in which it is mixed. Should you require it to set even more quickly, add a little salt to the water. This is somewhat of a disadvantage in some cases, as although you may wish it to set very quickly after it is poured over the object, sufficient time is not given for proper manipulation. I have therefore found it an advantage to sprinkle a cast with salt brine after it is poured.

Should the plaster in a vessel commence to set before you can use it do not attempt to soften it by the addition of more water. If this is done the plaster will not set properly and your work will be spoiled. Therefore, be careful and try to mix the right quantity and use it quickly. Should any be left over it is valueless and can only be thrown away. Always clean up tools after working or they will soon become rusted. Apart from this it is an annoyance to have need of a tool in a hurry and find it all stuck up with plaster or other material.

A Suitable Example

I have chosen to illustrate this lesson an ordinary potato, and the principles which I shall describe for the casting of that object are applicable with slight variations to almost any other.

The main thing in casting in plaster is to see that there are no undercuts, or places that would on account of their position prevent the cast from coming away from the object which has to be reproduced. In order that this may be successfully accomplished casts are made in from one to a hundred or more pieces. Large casts in which there are many pieces have to be made with a jacket. That is, after all the pieces are ready and in place, they are trimmed off smooth on the outside and thoroughly oiled, and a second cast is made over them to hold them in place. With casts that have only two, three, or four pieces, such as the one which I shall describe, this is not necessary.

The potato is placed upon its side in such a position as shown in Fig. 58. It has now to be built up around the edges in such a manner that the plaster will only be able to cover the exposed portion. Potter's clay is also good, and for larger objects a wall of sand nicely smoothed down is best.

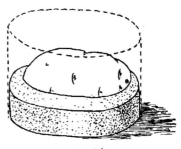

Fig 58.

The plasticine being built up as shown in Fig. 58 in such a manner that there will be no undercut, cut a strip of pliable pasteboard and tie it around the plasticine so as to form a fence about half an inch higher than the highest point of the potato,— the dotted line indicates the position. This is to retain the plaster. Any little openings that may be seen between the plasticine and the pasteboard inside must now be filled, and the exposed portion of the potato, upper surface of the plasticine, and inside of pasteboard, oiled. For ordinary work linseed oil or lard melted will do. For finer work I use olive oil. Next procure a bowl or suitable vessel and have it about one-third full of water, sift plaster into this until it heaps up in the middle, and stir until it is of a thick creamy consistency, avoid too many air bubbles. Pour this over the exposed half of the potato, and tap the bench smartly so that the plaster will settle into every place and give a correct impression of the object.

When this part is set, which should be in about fifteen minutes, remove the pasteboard fence, and

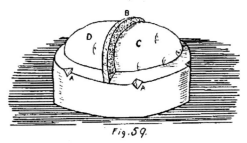

Fig. 59.

then the plasticine. This will expose the edge of the plaster. Now cut several V-shaped notches around the edge (Fig. 59).

On examining the potato let us suppose we find that if the remaining portion were cast in one piece it would not relieve properly on account of the position of the eyes. We proceed therefore to place a strip of plasticine in the position as shown in B. Now replace the pasteboard fence, raise it about half an inch and tie with string. Oil section 6 and the edge of the plaster and plasticine, and mix and pour plaster over that portion, being careful that none runs over D. Next re-

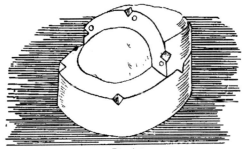

Fig. 60.

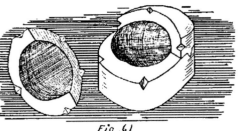

Fig. 61

move the fence and the strip of plasticine, and your cast will have the appearance of Fig. 60. Cut three notches as shown by O.O.O. Replace the fence, oil and cover the remaining portion with plaster. If properly done the cast should separate easily into three pieces, as shown in Fig. 61.

Now examine the inside of the cast for blow holes, and repair, by first saturating the inside with water and then filling the holes with a little plaster mixed with water. As previously stated the foregoing methods are applicable to all objects no matter how large, merely requiring a little intelligence on the part of the operator to adjust the portions correctly.

CASTING A FISH

The method of casting a fish is simply to imbed it to exactly half its depth in fine sand. This sand must be dampened so that it will be easy to smooth. The fins and tail are backed with potter's clay and pinned into place. The fish, first having had the mucus removed by sponging with water in which a little alum has been dissolved, is oiled. Plaster is then mixed to the consistency of cream, and poured over the fish. Personally I always build a fence of wood around it before I commence to cast, some, however, dispense with this and manipulate the plaster with a trowel or knife. The fence, I think is best especially when working alone.

The first coat having been poured entirely over the exposed portion of the fish and well shaken down, proceed to mix the next coat a little heavier and work in thoroughly some pieces of tow to bind it together. (This is essential in all large plaster casts.)

When the cast is of sufficient thickness, allow it to set thoroughly then remove the fence. Turn it over and lift out the fish, repair the blow-holes and set away to dry. Fish usually are cast only one-half and reproduced in paper, plaster, wax or other material and afterwards painted.

To make the cast of a deer head for use in making paper forms, the head, after being shaped as instructed for mounting heads, is coated all over with potter's clay and modelled nicely in every detail as it would appear beneath the skin. Make sure that both sides are alike and then cast as previously instructed.

FULL AND HALF HEAD CASTS

These are made in the same manner. The casts in all cases except where wax is to be used are repaired, allowed to dry thoroughly, and given two or three coats of shellac.

To take an impression in wax from a plaster cast, first immerse the cast in lukewarm water, and when still wet, pour in the wax. The knowledge of the proper temperature of wax for casting can only be gained by experience: the only information which can be proffered is not to have it too hot. (The proper stage of drying in which casts should be considered fit for this work is when they no longer appear slimy.)

CASING

It should be the aim of all taxidermists to try and case their specimens. Professionally this is often a difficult matter as the customer does not always wish to go to that expense. The amateur who is making a collection of trophies for himself has not this excuse, for apart from the cost of glass the expense is trifling. I am not taking into consideration the work which should be a pleasure in this case.

To my mind nothing is more annoying than to see a bird on which I had at one time expended a deal of care, all dishevelled, covered with fly specks and smoke. To me, it makes no difference that I was well paid for the work. It is, in truth, love's labor lost. It is therefore better for the amateur to do a few specimens and preserve them well than to amass a large collection that in a few years will be an eyesore and a ruin. Incidentally, such specimens are a bad advertisement.

One of the first essentials in casing a bird or animal is to have such embellishments as are used, as near as possible to those which would be found in its natural habitat. For this purpose the taxidermist should gather quantities of grasses, moss, ferns, lichens, etc., dry them and store them away in boxes. Grasses had better be gathered before they are fully ripe. They can be successfully tinted as needed by the sparing application of oil and powder colors. In using these it is better to put too little rather than too much, always remembering that the specimen is the principal object and keeping everything else subservient to it.

IMITATION SNOW

It is sometimes found necessary to represent snow. This is done as follows. Cover the parts necessary with a thick coating of flour paste, and with a shaker made of a tin with a perforated cover dust over thickly with equal parts of powdered alum and glass frosting.

A light frosted coating may be imitated on vegetation by dipping it into a strong solution of alum and allowing it to dry, when the deposited alum will crystallize. Glass frosting may be purchased from a dealer in taxidermist supplies, as may also artificial icicles made of glass. Should it be desired to represent deep snow, first cover the parts with fine cotton batting and then proceed as above.

To make artificial branches, stumps or small ground objects, first wrap wire about excelsior or tow to the desired shape and cover with the following composition—To equal parts of whiting and fine saw-dust add glue until it is of the consistency of thin mortar, to this may be added any desired powder color. It is best to have it dark to imitate the shadows in the crevasses of bark. Apply this to the branch and scratch it with the modelling tool or a splinter of wood. Do not be too particular in this operation or you will lose the desired effect.

When dry color the branch with powder colors and strong glue size, putting the color thickest on the highest places. It is essential in this class of work to have the shadows or crevasses very thinly painted and dark in tone, and the lights or high parts thickly painted and lighter in tone.

Rough rocks, etc., may be made in the same manner.

It adds greatly to their appearance to place birds and animals in some characteristic attitude. Owls, hawks, etc., as well as some carnivorous animals may be represented as devouring some species on which they prey, and for this purpose various small birds and animals that are too much damaged to make good specimens may be roughly stuffed and placed in the claws of the hawks, etc., and under the feet and in the mouths of carnivorous mammals.

Wading birds may be represented as standing or swimming in the water. For this purpose I have successfully used sheet celluloid, which I obtained from a manufacturer of automobile covers. Holes were cut to allow the feet or body of the birds to pass through and others punched for grasses, weeds, etc., the bed of the pool being first represented by making rocks, sand, mud, etc., by the processes previously described. I might remark here that it is of no use to model small pebbles: use the natural ones. The idea of modelling is to overcome weight.

While these few hints only touch upon the theme the reader will no doubt be able, with their help to devise many artistic combinations and groups. Much depends in this, as in other portions of the work, upon the artistic ability of the individual and his ability to observe.

COLORING AND TINTING

The proper use of color is indispensable to the taxidermist. The many hideously painted specimens one sees are indisputable evidence of this.

The colors commonly used by the taxidermist are ordinary powder colors for rough work which can be obtained from most any hardware or paint store, and artist tube colors (oil) for finer work.

The list of colors given on page 100, whilst small, will do for ordinary purposes if properly mixed.

A few combinations are as follows:

To Make   Use a Combination of:
Grey..........permanent blue—light red.
Grey..........ivory black—white.
Grey..........permanent blue—yellow ochre—vermilion.
Green.......chrome yellow—prussian blue.
Green.......ivory black—yellow ochre.
Green.......ivory black—chrome yellow.
Green.......permanent blue—chrome yellow.
Green.......permanent blue—yellow ochre.
Green.......Vandyke brown—chrome yellow.
Orange.....vermilion—chrome yellow.
Orange.....light red—chrome yellow.
Orange.....chrome (orange).

Many other combinations will suggest themselves as the reader progresses. It is better where fine work is required to use Cadmium yellow in place of chrome, it being much finer, more permanent and by no means so raw.

Before commencing to color a specimen see that the surface is properly cleaned. In painting the legs and feet of birds do not put the paint on so thickly as to hide the scaly appearance. In painting the bills, two or more colors often come together; see that the edges are properly blended, using a fine artist's brush for this. On larger surfaces an artist's badger softener is best. If the paint is to dry with a gloss, mix it with turpentine only; for a semi-gloss turpentine and linseed oil in equal parts; for an ordinary gloss add a little Damar varnish to the above; and for a high gloss use varnish alone to mix the color with or paint in the ordinary way and varnish afterward.

For coloring fish you will require additional colors. The following list I have found most useful, and for convenience I have divided them into two classes, the opaque and the transparent:

Opaque	Transparent
Flake white	Crimson alazarin
Zinc white	Purple lake
Naples yellow	Prussian blue
Chrome yellow	Brown pink
(light, med., orange)	
Cadmium yellow	Aureolin
(pale or deep)	
Yellow ochre	Gamboge
Light red	Bitumen
Raw umber	
Burnt umber	Olive green
Vandyke brown	Semi transparent
Ivory black	Burnt sienna
Vermilion	Terra Verte
Cobalt blue	

In coloring fish the most important thing to remember is to use as little color as possible. The white of the belly is better put on in two thin coats in preference to one heavy one which will destroy the demarcation of the scales.

When blending a transparent with an opaque color, as in the case of the jack-fish, where the white of the under parts joins and blends with the greenish tone on the sides, try and do it quickly and with as little mussing as possible, otherwise your work will have a muddy appearance.

With the exception of the under parts, transparent colors only should be used on scaly fish. Where there is a silvery or golden appearance, it can be imitated by using nickel or gold leaf as the case may require.

Gold size is applied to the parts, and when it is just a little sticky to the touch the leaf is applied. Experience only will teach the right method of using this material which is put on first and the color applied afterwards.

In coloring casts and models of fish, they are first given two coats of thin white shellac and then a coat of nickel leaf. In cases where the scales are not sharply defined each scale is lined with a very fine sable brush. The tone used in shading the scales is a grey composed of cobalt blue and light red. Coloring models of fish is a tedious process; I have spent several days on one fish but the effect is worth it. The fish is then tinted over same as the mounted specimen.

The best way to paint the bare skin of mammals, the wattles of some birds, etc., is to color them with oil colors mixed with turpentine and afterwards blend them with powder color of the same shade while the paint is wet.

To Paint a Glass Eye

Most glass eyes are purchased already colored. Flint eyes are sold for special purposes, these have the black pupil and the rest is transparent. They are painted on the back with oil colors mixed with Damar varnish. Most eyes are delicately veined, these veins are painted on first with a fine artist's sable brush, and the ground color put on after they are dry. In the case of fishes there is usually a gold or silver rim around the pupil. This must be put on first also, and next the ground tint.

Special hollow globes are sold by some dealers, these have no pupil. In this case the pupil is painted first, next the veins and lastly the ground color. With care an exceptionally fine job can be made in this manner, but for all ordinary work the colored eyes sold by the dealer in taxidermy supplies are all right.

The foregoing hints will be of little use to the student unless he makes up his mind to adhere closely to nature in all that he does, and to be patient and persevering, and satisfied only with the best that is in him.

It may also give greater confidence to know that a large proportion of Professional Taxidermists in this country took their first lessons from written instructions and gained proficiency by practice and observation.

The writer when a youth learned in this manner and, by working at the profession evenings earned more than he did at his regular business.

The student will also find many opportunities of doing likewise but must, of course, first attain some degree of proficiency in the art. Each job that leaves his hands is an advertisement, good or bad.

PRESERVATIVE SOAPS, SOLUTIONS AND OTHER
FORMULAS

In the practice of taxidermy various preservatives are necessary to properly cure the skins, tissues, etc., and render them as far as possible immune from the attacks of insects and decomposing agents.

That which is most universally used is arsenic, a deadly poison. It is however, compounded and mixed with other ingredients in such a manner that, used carefully it has no harmful effects.

For many years I was prejudiced against its use, and tried various non-poisonous preservatives, which while excellent in some climates and under certain conditions, are no good in this hotbed of moths and dermestes.

Regarding the use of arsenic and alum in equal parts, and in powder form, which is advised by some, I say distinctly NO, the particles of powder in the atmosphere cause a soreness in the nostrils, and must affect the lungs in a similar degree and also at one time of my life when I used this powder I was troubled with small ulcerations under the finger nails, no matter how careful I might be.

I finally decided to use arsenical soap and have done so for many years and found that if used with care it has no ill effects. The formula which is generally used is one advised by Horniday and others and is compounded as follows:

FORMULA 1

Arsenical Soap—(Horniday)
White bar soap..1 lb.
Powdered Arsenic........................1 lb.
Camphor ....2½ ozs.
Subcarbonate of Potash................3 ozs.
Alcohol ....4 ozs.

Directions—The soap should be the best quality

of laundry soap and of such composition that it can be reduced with water to any degree of thinness. Soap that becomes like a jelly when melted will not answer and should never be used. Slice the soap and melt in a small quantity of water over a slow fire, stirring sufficiently to prevent its burning. When melted add the potash, and stir in the powdered arsenic. Next add the camphor which should be dissolved in alcohol at the beginning of the operation. Stir the mass thoroughly, boil it down to the consistency of thick molasses, and pour into an earthen or wooden jar to cool and harden. Stir it occasionally while cooling to prevent the arsenic from settling at the bottom. When cold it should be like lard or butter. For use mix a small quantity with water until it resembles buttermilk, and apply with a common paint brush.

A very good soap can be mixed by simply taking one pound of good laundry soap, slicing it thin and then boiling as described, and afterwards stirring in one pound of powdered arsenic, whilst still hot. I prefer to do this in the open air, and not to hold the face over the pot while stirring. The laundry soap seems to contain sufficient potash or lye for all ordinary purposes. Camphor is not soluble in water and must always be dissolved in alcohol.

A solution which is of great value and is extensively used by professional taxidermists is compounded as follows:

FORMULA 2

Corrosive Solution

Corrosive Sublimate................1 oz.
Wood Alcohol.................1 quart

Corrosive sublimate (Bichloride of Mercury) is a deadly poison, and vessels containing it should be conspicuously labeled and kept out of the reach of children. It is best to have your druggist prepare the solution for you, and a much smaller quantity mixed in the same proportions will be sufficient. It is used to paint the skull, leg and wing bones of birds and animals that are to be mounted, and also to destroy moths and other insects that may be found attacking mounted specimens, it is applied in some cases with a brush and in others with a small syringe. In all cases use care in its use.

For the preservation of hides in a wet state, the salt and sulphuric acid pickle as given by Rowley is most extensively used by taxidermists. It is composed as follows:

FORMULA 3

Tan liquor for preserving hides in a wet state (Rowley.)

Water ....1 gallon
Salt ....1 quart

Bring to a boiling point to facilitate dissolving the salt. Add sulphuric acid (by measure) 1 ounce. Allow to cool before immersing hides. More salt, even a saturated solution will not injure a skin.

Many taxidermists advise the use of a solution of salt and alum for preserving hides, but I have found that the alum shrinks the skin to such an extent in some cases as to render its correct mounting almost impossible, and worse, the shrinking continues for a long time after the specimen is mounted, to such a degree as to break the stitches and cause other distortions.

It often happens that the taxidermist receives a specimen for mounting that is in a very advanced state of decomposition, with the hair slipping in places. The following pickle, also after Rowley is then very good:

FORMULA 4

Salt and Alum Pickle (Rowley)

Water ....1 gallon
Salt ....1 quart
Alum powdered or crystallized, 1 pint.

Bring to a boiling point and cool.

Hides that are very far gone may sometimes be saved by having this pickle quite warm, and then plunging in the hide and then turning and stirring to see that every part is saturated with the pickle, afterwards leaving the hide immersed for from 2 days to a week according to thickness, etc.

Probably one of the most useful compositions that is used by the taxidermist is Papier-Mache. For permanent work it has entirely superseded potter's clay and other compositions such as putty. It is prepared in a variety of ways. For ordinary work the following is perhaps the best:

FORMULA 5

Papier-Mache (Tose)

Make a quantity of paper pulp by tearing up and soaking pieces of common paper, afterwards rubbing it to a pulp. With some kinds of paper boiling will help. After it is thoroughly shredded squeeze out all surplus moisture with the hands. Now take a quantity of this pulp and add hot glue, in proportion about one of glue to three of pulp. Mix this thoroughly and then add plaster of Paris until the whole is thoroughly mixed and of the consistency of putty. The best method of mixing is to take a glazed earthen bowl, and, by pounding with a rounded stick gradually work the ingredients together in the same manner as a druggist uses a pestle and mortar. Should it be desired to color the mache, dry colors should be mixed in at the same time as the plaster. This composition will set more or less rapidly in proportion to the amount of glue used. It can be kept moist and workable for some days by wrapping in a damp cloth.

FORMULA 6

Papier-Mache (Tose)

Where a large quantity of papier-mache is to be used quickly, it is best made as follows:

Make a quantity of thick flour paste in a pail and stir in while quite hot pieces of fine paper. I always use the papers in which oranges and lemons are wrapped for this purpose, your grocer will save you a quantity, no doubt. This paper has the advantage of dissolving as it is stirred. Put in as much as the paste will hold. The best way to prepare this is to place a quantity on a board and with a trowel or large knife mix in Plaster of Paris until it is of the consistency required.

This has the advantage of being very inexpensive and is useful to cover large manikins and to make large masses of rock. Should it set too quickly it can be retarded by the addition of a little glue.

FORMULA 7

Papier-Mache, Fine (Tose)

A very fine papier-mache can be made as follows: Make a quantity of flour paste and stir into it fine paper. I usually use paper serviettes or towels, as they are of loose texture. Place a portion of this in a bowl and add Le Page's Liquid Glue and Dental Plaster, and mix thoroughly. This is an exceptionally fine modelling composition and can be tinted by the addition of powder colors.

Dental plaster is a very fine grade of plaster of Paris, and can be obtained from a dealer in dentist's supplies.

FORMULA 8

Gilder's Putty

The following composition is of great value where extreme hardness is required. If properly prepared it can be pressed into moulds and will take the finest impressions.

Glue, best white	1½ lbs.
Water	1½ pints
Resin	1 lb.
Boiled Linseed Oil	¼ pint
Raw Linseed Oil	⅛ pint

Soak glue in water and then boil in water bath (glue pot). Place resin in a separate pot and add the two oils, and melt. It is better to do this in a water bath, that is have the vessel that contains the resin mixture set in another with water the same as a glue pot. This last mixture is very inflammable and great care must be used in melting. When the resin and oil is thoroughly melted pour it gradually into the hot glue, stirring constantly. Now pour the whole mass into a larger vessel and add whiting. This must be finely powdered and entirely free from lumps. Mix and knead together while hot as you would dough. This composition can be kept a long time by placing in a box or jar, first moulding it into little cakes, and then covering it with whiting. When wanted for use it is placed in a steamer and softened. Pieces can then be cut off and pressed or moulded into any desired shape. This is the composition used for ornamenting picture frames.

FORMULA 9

Wax for mouths (Tose)

Bleached beeswax ....1 ounce
Paraffin wax ....2 ounces

Melt these together in a water bath. Place a small quantity of tube oil color in a spoon, fill with hot wax, and with a small palate knife or smooth piece of stick mix the wax and color. When well mixed hold the spoon in the melted wax and stir, the color will then mix evenly with the melted wax. Always melt in a water bath, otherwise the wax will burn and the color settle to the bottom. Should the reader have difficulty in making the wax combine properly he may overcome it by adding a greater proportion of paraffin wax, but this is not advisable on account of the low melting point of paraffin. Joins and laps in the wax may be smoothed by rubbing with a small piece of rag dampened with water.

For a good modelling wax I cannot do better than quote Montague Browne.

FORMULA 10

Modelling Wax (Montague Browne)

Common beeswax..............................4 ounces
Resin (finely pulverized)............2 ounces
Plaster of Paris................................½ ounce
Red Ochre Powder........................2 ounces

This is an ordinary dark red modelling wax, is tough and pliable, works well with the fingers, and unites readily without showing joints. The red ochre is merely added to color and may be substituted by any other powder color as occasion demands.

FORMULA 11

Flour Paste (Tose)

I find the best way to make flour paste is to place a vessel on the fire about one-third full of water and bring it to a boil. In the meantime mix a batter of flour and cold water in a separate vessel. When water is boiling stir in the batter gradually; this will make a paste free from lumps. A pinch of alum added to it will prevent it from souring for some time. Essence of cloves will also prevent souring and in addition gives an agreeable odor to the paste.

FORMULA 12

Arsenic Water for preserving mammal skins, etc.
(Horniday)

Water ....4 quarts
Arsenic .... 4 ounces

Mix, stir and boil until all the arsenic is taken up.

In closing it is perhaps well to issue a word of warning regarding the use of the various formulas containing poisons. They MUST in all cases be conspicuously labelled and kept out of the way of children. They must be used carefully and any cuts, sores or abrasions on the hands must be covered before commencing to use these preservatives. The finger nails must be kept·clean. These are precautions and there is no danger to the health if they are observed.

Printed in the United Kingdom
by Lightning Source UK Ltd.
130817UK00001B/79/A